Young

S0-CED-454

Adult

Ministry

Resources

Department of Education

United States Catholic Conference

In its 1987 planning document, as approved by the general membership of the United States Catholic Conference in November 1986, the Department of Education was authorized to provide leadership in young adult ministry and is, thereby, publishing a revised edition of *Young Adult Ministry Resources*. This document was reviewed by Sr. Faith M. Mauro, RSM, Representative for Youth and Young Adult Ministry and approved by Rev. Thomas G. Gallagher, Secretary of Education. It is authorized for publication by the undersigned.

Monsignor Daniel F. Hoye
General Secretary
January 4, 1988   NCCB/USCC

ISBN 1-55586-171-7

Contents

Introduction

The young adult population of today's Church is often a mystery to pastors, ministers, and parish leaders. Young adults are frequently the forgotten people of our Church, but they are also a source of many untapped gifts and talents. Young adults (eighteen to thirty-five years of age), single, married, or single again, are in need of recognition and attention. If we are going to be the Body of Christ in its fullness, the Church needs the energy, imagination, and perceptions that young adults have to offer.

In 1977, the United States Catholic Conference's Department of Education published *Young Adult Ministry Resources*. The book was meant to serve as a guide to those ministering to and with young adults. It offered insights into the developmental phases of young adults as well as expectations for the Church. Unfortunately, that 1977 book is no longer in print. On the recommendation of many in the field, a decision was made to reprint those chapters that are still pertinent to young adult ministry today; they have been incorporated into this present book. Those chapters will serve as a guide to all who encounter young adults and will assist those who wish to develop this valuable ministry. In addition, three new chapters have been included in this book. These chapters address key areas in ministry to, with, by, and for young adults: "An Open Letter to Pastors and Parish Personnel"; "Young Adults and Their Family of Origin"; and "Hispanic Young Adult Ministry."

Today's young adults are more diverse than ever before. There are more opportunities available to them in both Church and society. As ministers and leaders, it is important to be aware of these factors and to come to an understanding of the specific needs of the young adults in your local church and community. As you walk with them on this part of their life's journey, it is hoped that this book will serve as a valuable resource guide for developing a living and working ministry.

Sr. Faith M. Mauro, RSM
Representative for Youth and
Young Adult Ministry
Department of Education
United States Catholic Conference

Young Adults in Today's World

Who is considered to be a "young adult"?

Technically, adolescence begins with puberty and continues until the age of twenty-one. Therefore, one would presume that young adulthood would encompass the years from eighteen to approximately thirty-five. From the standpoint of ministry, however, we will use the term *young adult* to define an attitude and position in life rather than just age. It begins at that turning point in life when the young person actively assumes for the first time major decisions that previously were left to his or her parents. It may begin any time in adolescence and continue until the person has undertaken the responsibilities normal to mature adulthood. With this understanding, ministry with young adults would address itself to this role of decision making, which so fills their daily thoughts. Today's young adult must decide about a job, housing, money, sexual activity, and clothes while, at the same time, making more long-range decisions concerning education and the future of his or her life. The ability to meet these new responsibilities depends upon maturity, judgment, acquired skills, and previous experiences.

One aspect of our rapidly changing society is the fact that many young people at earlier ages are separating themselves from their parents. This split is evidenced in a breakdown of genuine communication; adoption of values differing from those of their parents; and, in many cases, physically running away from the family scene. When these young people reach young adulthood, they bring with them their experiences. In ministering with them, it is important to be sensitive and innovative.

In many cases, the young person's ability to function in this new role depends upon the psychological association with parents. Because of poor family relationships, many young people are prevented from making free, independent decisions for years, even after they have physically left the family circle. Quite often, the most difficult and traumatic experience for the young adult is breaking a dependency pattern with the parents. When gaining one's sense of individuality becomes such a struggle, it is understandable why young persons may also feel hostility for the Church, which is viewed as an extension of the value system life style of the parents. Learning how to live with newfound freedom, coupled with the responsibility of making important decisions, characterizes the life of the young adult. For many, the Church stands as a threat to both.

Commitment

In the adult world, commitments are very important. To make a commitment is to pledge oneself on a long-term basis, and to break that pledge is immoral. Adults join their Church and the Masons, Rotary, Lions, etc., for a lifetime, and they often attend religiously no matter how irrelevant and poor the programs. In addition to marriage, most commitments are to institutions and locations. In the past, adults have found the town in which they want to live, and then have found their work. They might work in one company all their lives, even if they never advance and the pay is unsatisfactory. Young adults, on the other hand, feel very mobile and have very little commitment to one place. The "place" is where you are in life. You can be who you are at any place. Technocrats may move from company to company, interested in making money to do what they want and to live as they want. Because of this mobile attitude of young adults, corporations are having to rethink the value of training programs, retirement benefits, and seniority status.

Commitment for the young adult means giving total involvement to an issue or idea. It means sticking it out to the end. What the young adult may see in the middle-class world are adults who subscribe to a series of partial commitments, none of which they are really willing to support all the way. "Movements" call for total involvement on a short-term basis. They are singularly oriented; their purpose is usually clear; the goal is direct. One can give to the movement for a number of months, knowing that when the task is accomplished, the movement will cease. Young adults understand this kind of commitment. Some understand more than short-term commitment, especially those in their thirties.

Religion

Ironically, at the very time when people are crying about the secularization of society, the new generation is focusing more and more upon basic religious questions. Yet, the number of young adults involved in the Church declines every year. The expressions of religion that have taken their unique shape in this country are largely a reflection of the older adult's understanding of life.

Many younger adults do not see the institutional Church today as bad, but simply unnecessary. Religion for them becomes the quest that is a part of every human life, that is, to discover the meaning of life. One young adult said to a group of older adults, "You can keep your dogma, your rational systems, your creeds, your edifices, but this doesn't mean that there is not spirituality in the universe." For most young adults, religion is important because it is synonymous with the search for meaning.

Conclusion

There is a conclusion that can be drawn from the above descriptions of today's young adults. If they are open about what they believe and how they think, they are not acceptable to the traditional, average church. Attempts to integrate these young adults into the typical community have led to serious conflicts. Most would rather stay away and be true to themselves than to undergo the pretense which they feel would be necessary. To accept this fact as reality is one key for opening the door of a relevant young adult ministry. It is more important now for the local church to have meaningful young adult ministries than it is to hold the concept that one community can be all things for all people, with everyone integrated into the "program" of the Church.

The Developmental Issues of Young Adults

The basic assumption of this section is that by understanding some of the developmental tasks and life issues with which young adults are dealing, we can more effectively plan for the ministry with them.

Most developmental theories propose stages of development. Each stage can be described by certain characteristics and a particular developmental task, such as identity or intimacy, which an individual must work through satisfactorily before entering the next stage. For most people, however, human development is not a clear-cut journey; our growth task may not be completely resolved before moving on to another.

Most of you are familiar with such names as Piaget, Erikson, and perhaps even Kohlberg. More recently, Gail Sheehy has published her book *Passages: The Predictable Crises of Adult Life* (New York: E. P. Dutton, 1976), which is material taken from human development theory and research on the age-specific thirty to forty year-olds.

Freud, Spock, and Piaget have charted almost every inch of childhood. Psychoanalyst Erik Erikson put the final touches on a convincing map of adolescence. Yet, until very recently, most of the charting stopped near the age of twenty-one—as if adults escape any sequence of further development. Now a growing number of researchers are surveying the adult life cycle.

The research so far has been narrow, concentrating largely on white, middle-class American males. (Editor's Note: Anita Spencer, in her book *Seasons—Women's Search for Self through Life's Stages,* is one of the few writers who has focused on the developmental cycles of a woman's life.) In separate studies, three of the most important life-cycle scholars—psychiatrist Roger Gould of U.C.L.A.; Yale psychologist Daniel Levinson; and Harvard psychiatrist George Vaillant—have reached some remarkably similar conclusions that add new dimensions to the topography of postadolescent life. The main features surfacing from their studies include:

Leaving the Family: (sixteen to twenty-two)

In this period, youthful fantasies about adulthood slowly give way. Young people begin to find their peers useful allies in an effort to break the hold of the family. Peer groups, in turn, tend to impose group beliefs. Emotions are kept under wraps, and friendships are brittle; any disagreement by a friend tends to be viewed as betrayal.

Reaching Out: (twenty-three to twenty-eight)

Following Erik Erikson, who found the dominant feature of the twenties to be a search for personal identity and an ability to develop intimacy, Gould, Levinson, and Vaillant see this period as an age of reaching toward others. The growing adult is expansive, devoted to

mastering the world; he or she avoids emotional extremes, rarely bothers to analyze commitments. To Levinson, this is a time for "togetherness" in marriage. It
is also a time when a person is likely to acquire a
mentor—a patron and supporter some eight to fifteen
years older.

Questions, Questions: (twenty-nine to thirty-four)

All the researchers agreed that a crisis generally develops around age thirty. Assurance wavers, life begins
to look more difficult and painful, and self-reflection
churns up new questions: "What is life all about? Why
can't I be accepted for what I am, not for what others
(boss, society, spouse) expect me to be?" An active social
life tends to decline during this period. Also on the
decline is marital satisfaction, and the spouse is often
viewed as an obstacle instead of an asset. Marriage becomes particularly vulnerable to infidelity and divorce.
Vaillant sees a crassness, callowness, and materialism
at this state. Levinson detects a wrenching struggle
among incompatible drives: for order and stability, for
freedom from all restraints, for upward mobility at
work. He says: "If a man doesn't start to settle down
by age 34, his chances of forming a reasonably satisfying
life structure are quite small."

Mid-Life Explosion: (thirty-five to forty-three)

Somewhere in this period comes the first emotional
awareness that death will come and time is running

out. The researchers see this stage as an unstable, explosive time, resembling a second adolescence. All values are open to question, and the mid-lifer wonders: Is there time to change? The mentor acquired in the midtwenties is cast aside, and the emphasis is on what Levinson calls "BOOM"—becoming one's own man (person). Parents are blamed for unresolved personality problems. There is "one last chance to make it big" in one's career. Does all this add up to disaster? Not necessarily. "Mid-life crisis does not appear to portend decay," says Vaillant. "It often heralds a new stage of person." The way out of this turbulent stage, say researchers, is through what Erikson calls "generativity"—nurturing, teaching, and serving others. The successful mid-lifer emerges ready to be a mentor to a younger person.

Settling Down: (forty-four to fifty)

A stable time: the die is cast; decisions must be lived with; and life settles down. There is increasing attention to a few old values and a few friends. Money is less important. Gould sees married people turning to their spouses for sympathy as they once did to their parents. Levinson notes that men tend to have fantasies of young, erotic girls as well as of older, nurturing women—all part of a final attempt to solve childhood problems and cut free from the mother.

The Mellowing: (fifty +)

These years are marked by a softening of feelings and relationships, a tendency to avoid emotion-laden issues, a preoccupation with everyday joys, triumphs, and irritations. Parents are no longer blamed for personal problems. There is little concern for either past or future.

Like Freud and Erikson, the life-cycle researchers argue that personality disorders arise when, for one reason or another, the orderly march of life stages is disrupted. Vaillant's studies suggest, for instance, that men who fail to achieve an identity in adolescence sometimes sail through life with a happy-go-lucky air, but never achieve intimacy, BOOM, or generativity. "They live out their lives like latency boys," he says, not mentally ill, but developmentally retarded at the childhood level.

The researchers' findings are tentative. So far, few members of minority groups or the working class have been studied, and the data on women is limited. Vaillant believes, however, that the female life pattern is much the same as the male's, except that the drive for generativity that appears in men in their late-thirties or early-forties may show up a decade earlier in women.

In any event, a thoroughly detailed portrait of adult life is still "many years away," as Gould concedes, and there is much skepticism in the academic world that one will ever appear. Yet, the life-cycle researchers are confident that the "threatening thirties" and the "mellowing fifties" will some day become as universally accepted as, say, the "terrible twos" and the "noisy nines" of childhood.

Getting to Know Young Adults

In order to locate young adults and be with them, one must move into the larger community to seek them out and befriend them. This must be done on a personal one-to-one basis. Announcements, written bulletins, and news media often will not reach or convene them. The very first call of the ministry is to go forth and meet young adults in their cultures, environments, and communities.

It is important to affirm that many of them, as they move away from family, Church, and other institutions, form their own extended families (living situations and relationships) and their own communities. They live in apartment complexes; and work, recreate, and vacation with other young adult friends. They live in the community cultures with which they identify.

It is important to emphasize the reality: the Church must go to them. We must seek them out and enjoy being with them, as Christ sought out the disenfranchised in his time, and, in his example, genuinely welcome them. We need to listen to them—they are adults—they must be taken seriously. Young adults will be the chief ministers of this ministry because they are adults and their baptism calls them to an active role in evangelizing themselves and their peers.

It would be wrong to go to them in the street culture, apartment complexes, prisons, bars, and other communities and implant a theology that only speaks in terms of "bringing Christ to them." Most young adults have not rejected Christ or their baptism but, in an era of substantial sociological change, have moved away from institutional religion. Christ is with them; we must discover how to see this more clearly.

The purpose of this chapter is to suggest some approaches for meaningful conversation and relationship with young adults.

1. *Serious Outreach*. The concept of "fisherman" is a salient reality of the gospel. It is more than a symbol or a way to make a living. We must go into the marketplace as men and women of faith and "reach out." This is essential to convening young adults. We must go with them, walk with them, and hear them. There must be a place for everyone. Indeed, nothing less than serious outreach, which is built on prayer, patience, and hopefulness, will be blessed. We must stay with young adults where they are, listening and learning. It would be wrong to reach out once and when they don't respond and follow immediately, to leave them. Our agenda cannot be to have them in the front pew of church next Sunday—nothing is instant; even conversion is a process.

2. *Welcoming*. This is a very important reality of the gospel and of our ministry. Christ reached out to everyone; he called and welcomed people. Welcoming assumes that we have prepared an environment to which we welcome persons. Young adult ministry must begin from within the community, the Church. We must help others to understand the special need of young adults and the diversity that marks young adulthood. The young adult culture is made up of many and varied

kinds of groups and subcultures; we must experience that diversity.

3. *Meal Ministry*. Christ always ministered to the human need. He was never removed from the practical concerns and struggles of people. If we read the life of Christ, focusing on the theme of meal ministry, we will soon realize how often the Lord ministered to people by feeding them. He convened, welcomed, and offered them hospitality. There are so many opportunities for us to do the same. It is deeply human to share our table of food, a symbol of the legacy Christ left us in himself. It is important to welcome and convene young adults around hospitality.

If a program is genuinely to reach out to young adults, it calls for the development of plans of ministry, projects, and programs to meet the particular needs of young adults in that environment. This special ministry attempts to manifest the word and deed of the gospel in the midst of need. Ideally, the young adult thrust is made by a team of three or more ministers, but this is not reality. Young adult ministers need to make contacts and build relationships with young adults. These contacts are made and relationships built through informal and formal visits to trade and business schools, colleges, medical centers, apartment houses, rooming houses, and other young adult gathering places. Almost any night these ministers need to be seen bringing the presence of Christian ministry to those who feel isolated, forgotten, and worthless. It is important that these ministers provide many hours of counseling to young adults who are concerned with drugs, suicide, jobs, marriage, rebellion, and vocation. Many of these persons have given up on society, family, and themselves.

Identifying Young Adults

If you wish to minister significantly with young adults in your particular community, you must find out who the young adults are; where they live, work, and play; what their needs, dreams, and interests are; where they are hurting. Only by surveying and experiencing *your own* community can you gather this information. And only after you have this information can you plan for relevant ministry.

A committee or task force composed of young adults can gather this information in several ways. They could

- collect information already in print (e.g., surveys, interviews);

- go out "on location" and experience the young adult world in all its diversity;

- talk with young adults and the adults who work with them; and

- be with them on a one-to-one basis.

The committee or task force could divide into subgroups, each of which would work on a different aspect of young adult life for a designated period of time. The subgroups would then report their findings to the total committee, which would use the gathered information as a basis for planning ministry with young adults. Two cautions: (1) Do not assume that a need is automatically the responsibility of the Church. (2) Do not assume that, if it is the Church's responsibility, it can be done without the help of other agencies and persons.

A process for gathering information might consider the following areas for subgroup investigation:

- *Housing.* Discover the various places young adults live. What housing is available to them? Is it readily available? What is the caliber of housing? At what prices? With what restrictions?

- *Jobs.* Who hires large numbers of young adults? How many jobs are available? What is the process of selection by employers? How do young adults feel about the employment opportunities in the community?

- *Education.* What are the educational opportunities for young adults (pay particular attention to trade schools, business schools, cosmetology schools, nursing schools, etc.)? At what cost? What controls are on students? What do students say about these schools? What are the employment opportunities after completion?

- *Social Service.* What agencies claim to serve young adults? What segments of the young adult population do they serve and how many? Interview several of these agencies. Talk with some young adults who have felt the impact of these agencies.

- *Leisure.* Where do young adults spend their leisure time (restaurants, record and book stores, sports events, night spots, vacation areas)? By all means visit some of these places and talk with both the proprietor and the patrons. Is there a large number of young adults who do not frequent any of these leisure spots?

- *Life Style.* What subcultures can you identify among young adults? What are their characteristics and values? Where do these groups intersect with each other and with other segments of the city? What are the conflicts and resolutions?

- *Young Adult Action.* How have young adults themselves responded to issues in government, education, housing, etc.? Through what channels do they act—community organization, new politics, old politics, underground media, unions, youth organizations?

At the end of the allotted time, compile the data from the subgroups into report form. Then hold a consultation to consider what this information says about ministry. What are the interests, dreams, issues, needs, and hurts of young adults indicated by this report? What kinds of response should be made?

Young Adults and the Church

In trying to reach young adults, churches need to be careful not to lose—through inactivity, disinterest, or neglect—those young adults currently involved in the life of the Church. It is important to remember that among those who say their attitudes toward religion have changed in recent years, many say they are now "more religious." It is, therefore, important for churches to continue to give spiritual direction to these newly involved adults in addition to ministering to those who have always been involved in the Church.

One's application of faith to his or her life is, of course, only as strong as the theological basis of this faith. If this faith is weak at the center, then all efforts and entreaties to reach young adults will likely fail. Recent survey findings indicate that certain basic beliefs are not held strongly and that religious practice is often intermittent. While 90 percent indicate they have had some religious training, it seems to have had little influence on their current theological perceptions. Perhaps, it behooves the Church to examine deeply the strength and basis of religious beliefs and practices. For example, it would be fruitful to explore the reasons people give for praying. Survey results show that responses under the heading of "petition" far exceed responses under the headings of "thanksgiving" or "intercession." It might also be valuable to explore rea-

sons for belief in God; one could certainly argue that few topics merit greater attention and study.

Many young adults participate only at the fringes of the Church, while many others are completely on the outside. The task of bringing young adults and the Church together for dialogue and meaningful ministry is an urgent one. The Church offers the good news of Jesus Christ, but it has not always been able to share the good news in ways that address the needs and concerns of young adults. The fact remains, however, that the gospel is relevant to the lives of all persons and to the lack of direction experienced by many young adults. On the other hand, the Church needs the energy, imagination, and perspectives that young adults offer if it is to be the Body of Christ in all its fullness.

Young adults who are apathetic toward their Church are not necessarily antireligious or anti-Christian. Many are genuine seekers. They are involved actively in their spiritual journeys, concerned with meaning in life and questing after something (or someone) to which they can commit their lives. In addition, one need only to look around our country to realize that we are in the midst of some type of spiritual revolution, in which young adults are chief participants. This heightened spirituality is evidenced by the Jesus Movement, the New Age, and the increasing interest in the occult. Within many Christian churches and seminaries, we can witness a rediscovery of the life of the spirit through liturgy, prayer, and personal confrontation with the Scriptures.

Styles of Ministry with Young Adults

Regular Parish

There has been a perceived decline of interest and participation by young adults in the life of the regular parish. This decline indicates the need for a radical rethinking of our approaches to young adults.

In working with young adults in a regular parish two considerations are important: (1) The physical presence of young adults at Sunday Mass or other liturgical services does not necessarily mean that the parish is fulfilling the needs of the age group. (2) Those young adults who actively join in parish-sponsored programs tend to be the ones who maintain values and perceptions held more by an older generation than those of their peers.

Strategic Parish

There are some parishes that, because of their location, spirit, facilities, and proximity to young adult communities, have strategic potential for ministry to young adults. Some of these are campus parishes, but here we are focusing on parishes that are located near large apartment complexes that cater to young adults; parishes in recreational areas that attract young adults; parishes close to business centers that employ large numbers of young adults; and parishes that, for no reason other than their spirit, attract young adults who live outside that parish. We refer to these as *strategic parishes*. We suggest that dioceses identify such parishes and that these parishes be encouraged to provide a wide variety of services needed by young adults, which are not feasible in every parish of the diocese. It is recommended that people who can relate easily to young adults be assigned to these parishes. This will probably require diocesan funding. The pastoral programs of these strategic parishes should reflect:

- the establishment of goals that assist young adults in their pursuit of self-awareness and Christian fulfillment; and

- a bringing together of diocesan resources to meet the unique needs of a young adult population.

A strategic parish would have no traditional parish boundaries, as we know them. It would be open and receptive to all those who wish to exercise their commitment to the community. For a strategic parish to properly function, it will require the employment and hiring of professionally trained, interested persons— both clerical and lay. It is recommended that the staff's educational backgrounds be conducive to the development of an interdisciplinary team ministry.

Missionary Effort

This perhaps is the most important effort. Today, there is a real need for missionary work with young adults. We are not suggesting specific forms, only emphasizing the need and encouraging experimentation. Such missionary efforts should involve clergy and laity, as well as utilize peer-group ministry.

Directions for Young Adult Ministries

Those communities that have begun to reach out beyond the traditional groups and develop new, relevant ministries have discovered certain directions. Though the styles of ministry are numberless, depending upon the place, the need, and the creative ideas of the inventors, there are certain common functions to which one can point:

The Listening Ministry. Listening means to tune in on the life of the community, to discover the real issues that are capturing the fears and imaginations of people. Listening is to discover when and where the gospel of compassion, reconciliation, and love is already active in the community. Listening means to know about the spiritual struggles that people undergo, especially when humans are being violated and justice stayed. In short, it is to give attention to the reality of the cross and resurrection in the daily lives of people.

The Ministry of Presence. It is quite possible to be in the community, to listen, and yet to be quite separate from its life. To be present is difficult to describe. It is to ask questions and take the answers seriously. It is to go in all manner of places without preconceived opinions and ideas. It is to identify with men and women in order to feel what they feel and experience what they experience. It is to saturate oneself, to enjoy oneself, to share suffering. It is to learn our own limitations and depend upon others for help. To be present is to discover the spiritual life of the community and to participate and become a part of it. At times, it is joining with those who protest, walking side by side or simply holding a hand. It is making oneself present to the world and, in so doing, making one's presence felt in the world.

The Issue-centered Ministry. One of the most significant aspects of young adult ministry is issue-centered or problem-oriented. These issues may range from those that concern young adults directly such as drugs, military service, and housing to such global and profound concerns as racism and world peace. The issues that capture the attention of young adults today draw them together, and the Church must discover its task in this framework.

Ministry of Linkage. The new generation has inherited a fragmented world that, in many ways, is becoming inoperative. In the areas of race, politics, education, and so forth, young adults are striving in new ways to break down the artificial barriers in society. The Church, by its very nature, needs to be an agent of reconciliation. Its ministry with young adults can serve as a link between young adults and their elders; between racial and ethnic groups; between heterosexuals and homosexuals; between conservatives and liberals; between runaways and parents; between the churched and the non-churched; between professionals and nonprofessionals.

Ministry of Enabling. One of the most admirable tendencies of many young adults today is the desire to create new ways for overcoming world problems. We see this in the many new movements and organizations involved with race, politics, sex, free speech, and education. In parallel with this initiative, there exists a sense of frustration leading to an eventual disillusionment. They are confronted by an adult world that does not take them seriously and generally discounts their ideas as being immature, especially if they are new and creative. Many young adults lack financial reserves and do not have the credentials and connections to acquire funds. There is a general feeling among young people that the structures of society are so tight that they are prevented from using "acceptable" methods to bring their ideas into reality. This sense of general frustration underlies much of the young adult unrest and protest. In truth, many of the proposals made by young adults are sound and innovative, with a high potential for success. Just as the new generation views world problems from a new perspective, so also is it able to see new possible solutions.

A new form of ministry is that of enabler. The enabler is an advocate, running interference, defending, supporting, and pleading the rights of young people. He or she begins with the affirmation that young adults possess many good insights and ideas and, if given the opportunity, can bring about elevating changes. This is a new role for the Church. This ministry calls on the Church to be more ready to cast its lot with those outside its fold who are attempting to improve human life.

Young adult ministries usually are vulnerable and subject to attack. The program-oriented congregation often presses, saying, "show us your program." The enabler does not possess a program of his or her own, but enables young adults to pursue their goals, without taking charge or absorbing their activities into the church structure. The young adults themselves make the final decisions. The advocate points the way, but does not lead by the hand.

The role of the Church as enabler is quite different from that of program operator. The distinction needs to be clear. For example: (1) As program operator, the Church has a vested interest in its own image, with a need to make its program run smoothly and a responsibility to see that financial contributions are wisely spent. (2) The enabler sees the opportunity for young adults to test their ideas as being more valuable than demanding that these ideas culminate in success. Therefore, failure must be allowed where decisions are poor and goals unrealistic. The following scenario depicts the Church as enabler: A group of young adults wanted to develop an information center for orienting newcomers to the city. The Church as enabler helped them obtain a grant from a private foundation and served in an advisory capacity. The young adults, through their own self-determination, did the rest.

There can be no "neat" conclusion to this chapter. It has sought to answer the question: How can the Church minister? Perhaps, it should end simply with an unanswered question: What will you do?

Young Adult Ministry Guidelines

The purpose of this chapter is to suggest direction for the implementation of an active young adult ministry and to define the areas of needed attention and action for the development of a viable and relevant program for the needs of Christian young adults.

The primary concern of the ministry is to present and extend effectively Jesus Christ as the center and source of young adult ministry; many young adults do realize that relationship with Jesus Christ. There is a need to extend this witness to other young adults in our communities. This can be done through attention to who, where, and what young adults are about today.

Some of the goals for this ministry need to be discussed and outlined. A young adult ministry can only have a realistic development when goals are developed and shared. It is also essential that, for program balance and effectiveness, there be a communication and information system that can provide data and draw resources from young adults; these two elements are starting points for this outline. One of the most important and essential factors involved in the development of a young adult ministry program is that of *advocacy* of the ministry. This advocacy may start in local church communities and extend to the diocese or vice versa.

Young adult ministry also needs to be a ministry "with and from" young adults. Leaders need to provide opportunities and offer direction and support. Persons in these communities are young adults—*not* youth—and it is important to treat them as such. They are capable of offering much to one another and to the community.

Young adults are living and moving in a learning society. All of life is a growing process. It is a period of development rather than transition. Ministry must be redirected to this life reality. The characteristics of independence, questioning, searching, and experimentation are common to almost all young adults. It is a development that needs to be expected and affirmed. There is a deep spiritual search among young adults. This special grace needs to be uplifted, celebrated, and shared. There are many gifts and many expressions, but one spirit.

Developing a realistic young adult approach demands that we have few immediate expectancies in terms of increased attendance or giving. Therefore, motivation must be found in long-range goals—in our own genuine concerns for others and the goals of evangelization.

There is no longer any basis for developing a "young adult social club" or a "Catholic singles club." Clearly, this social/recreational need is already provided for, and our energies need to be directed more clearly to ministry: being with young adults and listening, caring, and being a witness to God's love. However, a "group environment" can be one way to be with young adults.

There is a need to understand and appreciate the large diversity that defines young adults; they are not all alike. Nor are they simply to be defined as eighteen to thirty-five year-olds; chronological definitions are poor.

Faith Development and the Young Adult

It is an experienced fact that young adults go through a period when they suspend their belief, a time when previously learned beliefs are neither rejected nor affirmed, but held, as it were, at arm's length and sorted through or left dormant. It is a time not to do things that were once done, normative or expected, and to do things that were not done.

Many studies indicate that this period of suspension is pinpointed as occurring most frequently between the ages of seventeen and twenty-eight. Of all groups surveyed and interviewed on church belief and activity, this age category ranked lowest on personal piety, church activity, and need for religious absolutes. However, many of them did rank high on affirmation of their baptism and were found pursuing a serious spiritual search.

Christian educator John Westerhoff III, outlines four styles of faith in his work *Will Our Children Have Faith?* (New York: Seabury Press, 1976). They are (1) experienced faith; (2) affiliative faith; (3) searching faith; and (4) owned faith. Each is integral to itself, and one builds on and flows into the other. The process is *all of life*.

Seen as part of a process of development, *experienced faith* is dominant in childhood, as the individual learns through touch and experience to trust parental figures, the world, and God. *Affiliative faith* takes precedence in the school years in which one learns the story of his or her nurturing community. The individual depends on and derives identity from affiliation with the community of which he or she is a part. When faith continues to develop, there follows a period of *searching faith,* marked by questioning, experimentation, acting against the community, and commitment to various ideologies. As we have noted, the dominance of this faith style frequently begins in the late-teenage years. Provided that the needs of experienced, affiliative, and searching faith have been met, *owned faith* may develop as the predominant style, and the personal commitment and witness of the individual can strengthen the community.

The process of moving from affiliative faith to searching faith to owned faith is parallel to the movement from dependence to independence to interdependence in other areas of life. Late adolescence and young adulthood appear to be the usual times for the development of searching faith. For the young person who has been nurtured in the Church, this most often—if not always—includes a move toward independence from the Church and dropping out of church activities. Informal conversation with parish clergy and college chaplains gives the impression that over the past two decades a shift has taken place in the timing of this move toward independence. During the 1950s, it was common for students to cease active participation in church activities shortly after entering college, while at present, this often occurs before young people leave home. Studies indicate that those who remain active in church young adult groups are more likely to be dependent and more insecure than their contemporaries. Leaving active participation in church life seems to be part of a process of developing independence and searching faith.

However, what we see is the beginning of a process that frequently does not come to fruition. Individuals move into searching faith but do not come to owned faith. On the one hand, many reject or lose interest in faith, at least of a Christian variety. On the other hand, some return to the Church later, still seeking a dependent faith. Few persons appear to come to an owned faith within Christianity during the young adult years.

An Open Letter to Pastors and Parish Personnel

Ms. Brigid O'Donnell

Good Day!

You may be wondering why I am addressing this letter to you. I have worked with young adults for several years, and I have discovered over and over again how important priests and other parish personnel are in helping young adults feel and be a more vital part of our Church. So I write this to affirm you in what you are already doing and to encourage you to continue to be sensitive to the numerous needs of young adults. I have some practical suggestions that I have picked up along the way to share with you. But first, let's make sure we're coming from a similar understanding.

We are talking about young adults ministry, *not* young adult group. So often I hear pastors and parish personnel say, "We don't do anything for young adults." But in all likelihood, you do. A young adult group is one piece of young adult ministry, like one of the spokes of an umbrella. No one parish has all the spokes, but it can have enough to keep the umbrella open. We will take a look at what the various spokes are, but for now, think of yourself as being a young adult minister (among all the other hats you wear!). Being aware of and sensitive to young adult characteristics and needs may or may not add some responsibilities to your job/ministry. You will have to decide that. But it is hoped that it will make you more conscious of this important segment of our Church.

Who Are They?

Young adults are not an easy group to define. They range from post-high school age through mid-thirties, and include all the variations you can imagine:

- They are living at home or in their first apartment, buying a home, moving back home, moving to a new city.

- They are in college, in graduate school, voc-tech schools, going back to school after several years.

- They are single, married, divorced, separated, widowed, remarried, religious brothers and sisters, seminarians, priests, women and men.

- They are parents, single parents, single wanting children, single wanting no children.

- They are sexually active, in a permanent relationship, looking for a permanent relationship, not looking for a lasting relationship, celibate, straight, gay, and bisexual.

- They are in part-time jobs, unemployed, beginning a career, moving up the ladder, stuck in a job they don't like, changing careers, looking for a new job, underemployed, disillusioned with work, working in jobs that are satisfying but poorly paid, giving their lives in service.

- They are regular church goers, drop-outs, returnees, converts, searching, changing religion, agnostics, atheists, believers.

- They live in cities, suburbs, rural areas, prisons, treatment centers, barracks, dorms, tenements, hospitals, nursing homes, group homes, half-way houses, the streets.

- They are baby boomers (many of them), yuppies, poor, middle class, Hispanic, black, Asian, native American, Caucasian, and every ethnic group known.

- They speak English, English as a second language, or only their native tongue.

- They are handicapped, mentally ill, mentally retarded, deaf, socially maladjusted, in AA or Al-Anon, coping with drugs or terminal illness.

And the list goes on. I mention some of these characteristics to point out that it is impossible to describe accurately such a diverse group of people. It also shows how difficult it is to fashion a ministry for so wide a population. You already know many of the people you serve in your parish. Some of the young adults I described are not members of your parish. Some could be if you reach out; some will never fit into your community. Some may reach out to you; some need to be welcomed.

- Do you know who the young adults are in your parish? If you were to list them, would any group be missing?

- Did you include members of your parish staff (perhaps the youth minister, teachers, principal, DRE, associate pastor, pastoral minister)?

- Did you remember the college students who are home only at holidays and during the summer?

- Did you include the volunteer catechists, musicians, youth workers, committee members, lectors, ushers, and eucharistic ministers?

- How many single young adults are members of your parish community?

These questions are not meant to overwhelm you or make you feel guilty. Rather, they should help you identify the young adults in your parish; show you how you already are ministering to and with them; and, perhaps, give you some ideas about where to reach out to them.

Two characteristics of young adults often make reaching out difficult. First, *young adults are very mobile*. When doing address corrections on a YA Newsletter mailing list of 2,400, I found that 600 of those on the list had moved in one year—that's 25 percent. Or young adults may be in your parish one weekend, at a friend's the next, on vacation a third week, and so forth. Second, when young adults do come to your parish, *often they don't register,* thereby making it difficult to have an accurate count or to send out invitations. There are no real solutions to these dilemmas, but being aware of them can lessen some of your frustration in reaching out, especially to single young adults.

Having said all that, it's also important to understand the different stages of young adulthood. (For more detailed information, see D. Levinson's *The Seasons of a Man's Life* and A. Spencer's *Seasons: Women's Search for Self through Life's Stages*.) Each stage has different tasks and different needs.

Early Adult Transition (seventeen to twenty-two, approximately)

Two tasks:

1. Move out of the pre-adult world:
   - question that world and one's place in it;
   - modify or terminate existing relationships with important persons, groups, institutions; and
   - reappraise and modify self.
2. Make preliminary step into the adult world:
   - explore possibilities;
   - imagine self as participating in the adult world;
   - begin formulating adult identity; and
   - make and test some preliminary choices for adult living.

Of particular note for you is that early young adults modify or terminate existing relationships with important persons, groups, institutions. The young adults who were active in the youth group may make themselves scarce, not because they don't care, but because they're modifying or terminating that relationship with the Church.

First Adult Life Structure (twenty-two to twenty-eight, approximately)

Chief task: make a provisional structure.

They will make and test a variety of initial choices: occupation, love relationships, friendships with peers, values, life styles, and so forth.

Two tasks (pull against each other):

1. Explore the possibilities:
   - options open;
   - no strong commitments;
   - maximize alternatives;
   - adventure and wonder.
2. Create a stable life structure:
   - become more responsible;
   - make something of one's life.

You can see many possibilities for ministry with this group, can't you? Help in discovering values, in making vocation and life-style choices, and in finding new friends are just some of the opportunities to minister with these young adults. Perhaps, meeting others who are struggling with the same issues and questions is one of the best services a parish can offer young adults in this stage of development. More on that later.

Age Thirty Transition (twenty-eight to thirty-three, approximately)

1. Reappraise past and consider future:
   - What have I done with my life?
   - What do I want to make of it?
   - What new directions shall I choose?
2. Provisional exploratory quality of the twenties is ending:
   - life is more serious, more restrictive, more "real";
   - second chance to create a more satisfactory life structure.

People handle this stage in different ways. They may modify what they have been doing; enrich it; make a life structure that is based on the previous one but is very different; continue as they are; or know that something needs to be changed but are not be able to do it. Generally, there is a move toward major new choices or a recommitment to existing ones.

In my experience, this stage is especially difficult for the single young adult who wants to be married, and very painful for women who want children and who hear their biological clocks ticking away. It can also be a time of career/job changes, divorce, or other significant life-style changes.

As ministers, you can be present to listen and to help guide young adults in this transition, to let them know the Church cares about and has a place for them.

But the picture isn't complete with only this view of young adults. We need some other dimensions.

What are they looking for? According to Daniel Levinson, young adults have four major tasks: (1) forming a dream and giving it a place; (2) forming mentor relationships; (3) forming an occupation; and (4) forming love relationships.

Let's look at each of these tasks and see what role you as a church leader can play in ministering with young adults.

Dream

The dream can be many things. Whatever it is, the young adult strategizes ways to accomplish it. Do you give suggestions about what to include in the dream? Our American consumer society plants many ideas about being successful, rich, beautiful, and so forth. The gospels are filled with dream possibilities: "Whatever you do to the least of these. . . ."; "Go, sell all you have. . . ."; "Love the Lord your God . . . and your neighbor as yourself . . . the pearl of great price. . . ."

and on and on. What role does the gospel have in the dreams of young adults? What ways can you think of to broaden the formation and fulfillment of their dream?

Mentor

A mentor is someone several years older and is a person of greater experience and seniority. That person is a teacher, sponsor, host, guide, exemplar, counsel, and provider of moral support. The mentor represents a mixture of parent and peer.

Young adults find mentors in schools and in jobs or careers, but where is the mentor in the church community? Two good examples are marriage preparation done with an older couple and the RCIA. Both of these examples set up a structure that pairs a seeker of truth with an older person(s) with whom the young adult can identify and who is willing to be a sponsor (mentor).

The challenge comes for young adults who are not married or entering the Church. To whom do they turn for guidance on their spiritual journey? Some seek out a spiritual director or a person on the parish staff, but that is the minority. Is it possible for parishes to set up a mentor process for young adults? And if not a process, is the staff approachable so that young adults can come with their questions? Much food for thought!

Occupation

Since most of us spend a great deal of time in our occupation, it is important that we see its worth. The Church has long honored the dignity of work. Do you do a good job of linking work and spiritual life, pointing out the importance of the Christian in the marketplace? Is there a way to help young adults work through value conflicts that sometimes arise at work? While we are more than what we do, what we do is valuable, no matter what the job.

Perhaps, a homily or two on this topic will speak not only to young adults but to everyone in the community. In addition, recognizing volunteer work done in the community (not just the parish) is another way of saying that there is spiritual life and growth outside the parish doors.

Love Relationships

For many people, marriage and family are part of the dream, and young adults probably account for most of the weddings in your parish. You already know the ministry involved in marriage preparation and the ceremony itself. A marriage can be a time of welcome to young adults, a personal invitation to be a part of the parish community, or it can be a real turn-off. If all you do is concentrate on making this life experience a good one for the couple and their friends and relatives, you are involved in young adult ministry.

But not everyone gets married. Other relationships—both romantic and nonromantic—need to be nurtured. Where in the Church can young adults form those bonds? Sometimes, it is in a group. (More on that later.) Sometimes, it is by volunteering in the parish community (musician, catechist, etc.). Or it can be by participating in a Eucharist, which is vibrant and prayerful, where they can feel one with the faith community and, perhaps, even form some friendships. If Sunday Eucharist is a mediocre experience, you can be sure the congregation will lack young adult faces and voices.

Erik Erikson, in his book *Childhood and Society,* identifies two stages of young adulthood that confirm what has just been said. In the struggle of *intimacy vs. isolation,* the young adult asks: "To whom am I significant?" and in *generativity vs. stagnation,* the person asks: "To whom can I give myself?" These questions are not single or married issues and, obviously, have multifaceted answers, but a parish community can provide some possibilities when a young adult asks them.

What are young adults looking for? In terms of faith, most likely they are searching. Using John Westerhoff's terms (*Will Our Children Have Faith?*), they have probably moved from *affiliative faith,* where authority rests in the community and the person focuses on the tradition for continuity, order, stability, and well-being, to *searching faith.*

In searching faith, persons are concerned about establishing personal consciousness in terms of beliefs, attitudes, and values, looking for membership in a community that can explore reality without losing it. They look for persons and ideas in which to have faith. Authority shifts from the community to self. They need to have a vision, a purpose for life, to influence their environment. They look to the future and reshape tradition through critical judgment. Searching faith is dominated by an intellectual way of knowing.

According to Westerhoff, leaving active participation in church life seems to be part of developing independence (also a trait of young adulthood) and searching faith. Some leave entirely. Some leave by being physically present at Eucharist but not being involved in any other way. Some ask the questions out loud, while others ponder them within.

What happens to young adults in searching faith? Some avoid the questions and issues and go back to a dependent, affiliative faith. Some find the answers in other churches. Some drop out completely. Some never resolve the quandary and go on somewhat aimlessly. And some move into *owned faith,* where authority is in transcendent principles and norms and the paradox of continuity and change is recognized but not resolved.

The Church has a hard time recognizing and affirming searching faith. It looks like doubt or unbelief, and many people are uncomfortable with uncertitude. Many adults in the Church have not gone through searching faith themselves, so they hardly can welcome the searchers, who threaten their affiliative faith.

What can you, as a church leader, do? First, recognize your own faith search and acknowledge it. Welcome young adults with their questions. Just how to do this is a tough issue, but sometimes young adult groups provide an entry in a nonthreatening way. Being or providing a mentor is another good way. Much of young adult ministry is one-to-one, not a group. Be someone young adults can approach with their doubts and questions. Be nonjudgmental; remember, they're looking for the truth. For those young adults who have moved into owned faith, provide ways for them to share their insights. Invite them to teach, to be an RCIA sponsor, to be a parish minister, or to share their story with other young adults.

What do we provide young adults who have searched and decided to come home? How do we welcome them back? Again, reflect on those two questions: To whom am I significant? To whom can I give myself?

Those churches that attract large numbers of young adults are the ones with a strong community, filled with friendly, outgoing people and opportunities for service. Some churches attract young adults because they also give clear-cut answers to their questions. Because so much else is changing in young adults' lives, they may be looking for that security. Although we cannot give them that guarantee, we can share our own stories of struggle, insight, and faith.

Group

As you have already seen, the young adult group is only one component of young adult ministry. It can, however, be an important way of meeting young adult needs in your community. Sometimes an area-wide group has more potential members and is easier to sustain. The group should have a statement of purpose and be clear about who is welcome to come. Some groups are for married and single young adults, while others invite only single young adults. Most groups advertise for people between the ages of eighteen and thirty-five, with variations on the specific age range.

A core team of three to six people help plan and organize the direction and activities of the group. This is not a club, so usually there are no officers or dues. Members can be asked to contribute money to defray expenses, and often the parish allocates some funds for printing a newsletter, mailings, and other administrative costs. All activities should be self-sustaining, especially social ones. The group may have a parish budget for speakers, staples, and retreats. If the parish sees the group as part of its ministry with and to young adults, it makes sense to spend some money to give it the quality it deserves.

Young adult groups that have a liaison with the parish staff are more conscious of their place in parish life, and the staff is more aware of young adults. This liaison need not be present for all planning meetings or activities, but may attend some of them for visibility and to show that the Church is sincere in its care for young adults. If young adults form a relationship with the staff person, it can pave the way to pursuing deeper issues and offer young adults the possibility of cultivating a mentor. The staff person can also refer young adults to others who may better meet their needs. Don't underestimate the kinds of discussions that occur over coffee or pizza after the volleyball game; they are great opportunities for young adult ministry!

The core team is charged with peer ministry, in an informal way, as well as with planning and organizing. They are the ones to set the atmosphere at events, to reach out to the newcomer, to welcome everyone, and to provide hospitality. If they see what they're doing as "ministry" rather than "group planning," the group will be more than a social get-together. A staff person might work with the core team to help them gain or strengthen ministry skills. Core team members should change periodically to prevent burnout and to keep the group from being identified with one person.

Young adult groups include four elements: (1) educational spiritual growth; (2) prayer; (3) service; and (4) social. The main objective is to build community, to form relationships. The group should offer a variety of things, not just social/recreational. And to prevent disappointing members, group activities should be somewhat limited—maybe two or three per month—at least until there is a high number of participants. With too many things to choose from, activities draw small numbers or attract mainly those whose social lives revolve around the group's calendar.

While this is not an extensive description of a young adult group, it gives you some ideas of how to get started.

What Is Ministry with Young Adults?

First of all, ministry with young adults is *not* a program. You may offer some programs, but they are not the heart of young adult ministry. The heart is *relationship*. It is building relationships among young adults. It is enriching and enhancing young adults' relationships with themselves. It is helping them discover or rediscover their relationship with God and Church. It is offering opportunities to build relationships with the parish community, the workplace, the civil community. It is finding mentor relationships for young adults. It is helping them find relationships between faith and life. It is essentially one-to-one.

Often, ministry with young adults is planting seeds. It is nurturing dreams, rejoicing in accomplishments, helping in transitions, holding the candle in the tunnel of doubt, grieving over losses in relationships, clarifying values, challenging growth, loving the sinner, discovering potential, and encouraging generosity. It is being in the right place at the right time. It is being oneself and being open.

It is a ministry of presence: touching their lives; a ministry of listening: hearing their story; a ministry of healing: bringing compassion and care to the suffering; a ministry of liberation: being freed from personal and communal oppression; a ministry of integration: finding roots and continuity. Ministry with young adults cannot be measured by numbers in a group, or weddings, or appointments on calendars. It can only be measured by the heart.

Practical Strategies

I have given you some suggestions along the way, but let me elaborate further:

- *Provide scripture study for young adults.* Many other Churches offer this type of group, which not only answers biblical questions but also provides an entree for other questions of faith, as well as companionship for the participants.

- *Invite young adults to join you.* Ask them to become members of the education and finance committees, parish council, liturgy planning committee, and so forth. Many young adults are in responsible positions where they work and can bring not only their expertise but a different perspective on issues.

- *Have a social event at the parish.* When college students are home for vacation, schedule a social event. It's a sign that they are still welcome and belong, and an opportunity for them to be reunited with high school friends.

- *Offer an evening on being Catholic.* Young adults can come with their questions and gain insights into why it is important to continue to be an active church member.

- *Arrange periodic meetings for specific segments of your community.* Invite newly married couples or people who have recently had their babies baptized to meet with one another. Have experienced couples or parents there to give guidance and support. Make it social as well as educational.

- *Give good homilies.* Use examples that include everyone, especially those who are single. Use inclusive

45

language. The homily is the time when most people connect with the priest.

- *Pair up new parishioners with old.* When young adults join your parish, pair them up with other single or married parishioners. The seasoned parishioners can make the newcomers feel welcome and perhaps form new friendships. Singles especially will like to know someone else in the parish.

- *Have information available on young adult groups.* It is important for the the parish secretary to know where to direct young adults who call to inquire about a young adult group. If the parish has such a group, the secretary should have the name of the contact person and his or her phone number. If the parish has no group, it is important that the secretary know where to direct the call, perhaps to the diocesan contact person.

- *Set up a listening session.* Schedule a time and place where young adults who wish to voice their concerns about the parish, the Church, etc., will have a forum to do so.

- *Give them a break.* Single, young adult parents often need a respite. Arrange for high school youth to baby-sit free of charge.

- *Propose ongoing communication.* Suggest to young adults in RCIA that they continue to meet after the Easter Vigil and Mystagogia. The bonds of community are already there and can be strengthened without much more than a suggestion from you.

- *Provide opportunities for questions and answers.* Young adults who marry or have a child baptized often have questions or concerns that involve the Church.

Provide an opportunity for them to voice these questions and concerns.

- *Make "being single" a positive vocation.* Do not omit the single life when speaking of vocations. Even though many young adults are single, a good number of them dream of being married. Some young adults will *always* be single and presenting this as a positive vocation will help them to accept the single life as a gift rather than a disappointment.

Plan of Action

If you have read this far, you probably are thinking, "How can I do all those things?" You can't. You need to be selective and trust that in your parish community there are gifts enough to serve everyone. It is hoped that this letter has expanded and deepened your understanding of young adults and young adult ministry. What you *can* do is share this letter with others on your staff. You can be more conscious of young adults in your parish. You can use a staff meeting to explore how you already minister with young adults. And you can choose one new way to touch young adults. It may be one of the things suggested here; it may be another creative venture. Nothing is too large or too small.

Young adults are not the future of the Church. They are vital members and leaders of our faith communities now. They bring with them all the enthusiasm and idealism of young adulthood. We need their insights and challenges as much as they need the wisdom of mentors and tradition.

Godspeed in your ministry with young adults!

Selected Resources

Fee, Greeley, McReady and Sullivan. *Young Catholics*. New York: Sadlier, 1981.

Gribbon, Robert T. *One-Half the Congregation*; *30 Year-Olds and the Church*; and *The Problem of Faith-Development in Young Adults*. Washington, D.C.: The Alban Institute.

Gura, Carol. *Ministering to Young Adults*. Winona, Minn.: St. Mary's Press, 1987.

Hershey, Terry. *Young Adult Ministry*. Loveland, Colo.: Group Books, 1986.

Hoge, Dean R., et al. *Converts, Dropouts, Returnees: A Study of Religious Change among Catholics*. Washington, D.C.: USCC Office of Publishing and Promotion Services, 1981.

Levinson, Daniel. *The Seasons of a Man's Life*. New York: Ballantine Books, 1978.

Ohanneson, Joan. *And They Felt No Shame: Christians Reclaim Their Sexuality*. New York: Winston-Seabury Press, 1983.

Parker, Sharon. *The Critical Years: The Young Adult Search for a Faith to Live By*. New York: Harper and Row, 1986.

Spencer, Anita. *Seasons: Women's Search for Self through Life's Stages*. Mahwah, N.J.: Paulist Press, 1982.

Whitehead, Evelyn and James. *Christian Life Patterns: The Psychological Challenges and Religious Invitations of Adult Life*. New York: Image Books, 1982.

Young Adults and Their Family of Origin

Rev. Thomas Lynch and Sr. Faith Mauro, RSM

The role and position that young adults play in their family of origin will always have a major influence on how they relate to others:

> This unique position can dilute or nourish natural strengths; it can be a dragging weight that slows our progress throughout life, or an additive that enriches the mixture of our propelling fuel. The more one understands that position, therefore, and the more one can learn to occupy it with grace and "savvy," rather then fleeing from it or unwittingly allowing it to program our destiny, the more effectively one can function in other areas of life.[1]

This chapter will address the interconnection between young adults and their family of origin. First, this dynamic will be addressed by examining the normal life cycle of the family, with its implications for young adults. Second, the young adults' parents' pattern of interaction will be examined to see how these patterns affect how young adults will relate to other men and women. Third, the way the family as a whole interrelates will be examined to help determine the kinds of communities to which young adults will be attracted. Fourth,

---

[1]E. Friedman, *Generation to Generation: Family Process in Church and Synagogue* (New York: Guilford Press, 1985), p. 34.

the young adults as change-agent in the family of origin will be examined.

The insights in this chapter regarding young adults and their family of origin are not meant to be taken as absolutes. They are meant to help young adults review their family of origin from a different starting point. Many times, young adults get caught in viewing their family of origin from only one perspective. A new starting point may help young adults to become engaged with their family of origin in new ways and, therefore, free them to enter healthier and more life-giving relationships in the other spheres of their lives.

Family of Origin

To begin with, it is important to have an understanding of what is meant by one's "family of origin." One's *family* is that "intimate community of persons bound together by blood, marriage, or adoption for the whole of life."[2] The *family of origin* refers, in particular, to the family into which one was born or adopted. It includes the parent(s) and sibling(s) plus extended family (grandparents, aunts, uncles, cousins). One's family of origin has "specific patterns of behavior, perceptions, and thinking, as well as specific issues, for example, sex, money, territory, drinking, separation, health. These have an uncanny way of reappearing."[3]

It is important for young adults to realize that these specific patterns of behavior, perceptions, and issues

---

[2] Ad Hoc Committee on Marriage and Family Life, National Conference of Catholic Bishops, *A Family Perspective in Church and Society: A Manual for All Church Leaders* (Washington, D.C.: USCC Office of Publishing and Promotion Services, 1988), p. 8.
[3] Friedman, pp. 31-32.

have a major influence on how they enter and develop relationships. When the young adults recognize that these behaviors, perceptions, and issues are transmitted from generation to generation, then they are able to identify and come to terms with the experiences of their family of origin. This process of identification and ownership assists young adults to be free of the baggage encumbering them, thus enabling them to choose how they will live in relationships.

The Family Life Cycle

The family life cycle is a natural process that involves a series of stages through which a family moves during the life of that particular family. It begins with marriage and is repeated generation after generation. Each stage has a particular beginning, and family members may be involved in several stages at the same time. "In each stage, a family has particular tasks to accomplish and challenges to face in order to prepare itself and its members for growth and development."[4] At each stage of its development, the family and its members have to readdress how close or how separate they are going to be to one another. The family also needs to focus on how flexible or how structured their family life will be. The structure that was developed at one particular time of the life cycle may need to be adjusted so that the family can more effectively function. "A new stage . . . is reached when [a person or married couple] is required to function in a new role, using information and skills that were not used or needed previously."[5] A knowledge

---

[4] *A Family Perspective,* p. 26.
[5] D. Guernsey, *A New Design for Family Ministry* (Elgin, Ill.: David Cook Publishers, Co., 1982), p. 42.

of these stages will help young adults understand the complexity of their family life. It will assist them in realizing the tasks that need to be undertaken so that young adults and their families may move successfully through each given stage.

The stages of the family life cycle, as identified in the National Conference of Catholic Bishops' manual for pastoral leaders *A Family Perspective in Church and Society* (Chapter Five) are as follows:

1. *Establishment: new family without children.* This is the time for the newly married couple to become a separate, but connected unit of their family systems.

2. *New Parent(s): couple or one parent with one or more under-school-age child(ren).* This is the time when a new family moves to establish new subsystems: parent-child and sibling-sibling.

3. *School-Age Family: couple or one parent with school-age child(ren) and/or adolescents.* This is the time when a family needs to foster individuation and the growth of each of its members. This task frequently intensifies when children enter adolescence. At this time, the family needs to promote individuals' increasing independence while redefining family participation.

4. *Empty-Nest Family: couple or one parent during and after child(ren) leave home and/or enter the productive sector; middle-age couple without child(ren).* This is the time when a family begins to regroup, and relate to each other and new members (in-laws) on an adult-to-adult basis.

5. *Aging Family: couple or one parent after retirement.* This is the time when a family deals with issues of retirement, death, role reversals, reinvestment, and diminishing financial and physical resources of the older members.

Individuals can be in different stages of the life cycle with different generations. For example, a young adult can be in the New-Parent Stage, while his or her family of origin is in the Empty-Nest Stage. Whether young adults are single, married, or single again (widowed or divorced), it is important for them to be aware of the different tasks that they need to initiate. This awareness will assist them in successful negotiation of the different stages with their family of origin and free them to establish healthy relationships.

In this section, particular stages of the family life cycle will be examined with their implications for young adults. These will be the Empty-Nest, the Establishment, and the New-Parent Stages.

Empty-Nest Stage

Young adults initiate their family into the Empty-Nest Stage by leaving the home for college, work and/or to establish a residence by themselves. The parents now need to relate to young adults in a new manner. As young adults now take greater responsibility for their lives, the parents seek ways to let go of their need to parent and try to relate to their children as adults. This is often as difficult for the young adults as it is for their parents.

When young adults leave the home, there is a vacuum. Often the parents need the young adults to fill part of their lives so as to avoid addressing the issues of the ongoing relationship with their spouses and/or other relationships. Their lives, since their children were born, often have been centered around the children. Now the parents need to establish new ways of relating with their spouses and others. This establishment is often difficult and may strain their relationships until they work out a new way of relating. Parents may realize that they have very little in common with their spouses or other relationships. They also may experience depression and an acute sense of loneliness. Sometimes parents do not want to undertake this task, and they cling to the young adults, often making it difficult for young adults to grow up. It is important for young adults to be aware of these dynamics so that they do not become emotional hostages between their parents.

Sometimes young adults are unable to let go of their parents. Young adults continue to engage in false starts in adulthood and, after awhile, flee back to the safety and protection of the nest. In this dynamic, young adults may play on the parents' inability to let them go and set up a situation were the parents take responsibility for their children's lives. This may take place whether young adults are living on their own or in the home of their parents. In the parents' home, this is manifested by young adults taking very little responsibility for the running and maintenance of the house. When young adults are living on their own, this dynamic is exhibited by the children continually handing over to their parents some of the daily responsibilities (e.g., meals, laundry, bills). They believe that their parents will bail them out if things go wrong. The parents also may fall into the role of taking care of the young adults, even though they complain about doing it. Young adults and their parents are feeding off each other's neurotic needs so that both do not have to face the issues at hand: the parents' letting go of their children and reestablishing new ways of relating with their spouses or others; and the young adults taking responsibility for their own lives.

There is another dynamic that may begin at the start of the Empty-Nest Stage and can extend throughout the life of the single young adult. It is pressure from the parents to marry. This pressure may take many forms and may heighten young adults' feelings of being unloved and unwanted. In a situation such as this, parents find it difficult to let go and let their children grow up. The following underlying attitudes are present: a woman needs a man to take care of her; a man needs a woman for rootedness; once young adults marry they will be okay—all grown-up. These dynamics eat away at the young adults' self-confidence because, in reality, parents are saying, "Stay home, you can't make it on your own."

As leaders assisting young adults with the different dynamics of the Empty-Nest Stage, it is important to help them take responsibility for their own lives and to free themselves from the expectations of their family of origin. One way to do this is through awareness. It is also helpful to assist young adults to focus the issues in order to see clearly what they need to do. Taking time to work out some plans of action may help young adults move from awareness to change. In this move from awareness to change, the support of leaders/ministers is critical, especially in the initial steps.

Establishment Stage

When young adults enter into the covenant relationship of marriage, they need to develop new ways to relate to their family of origin. These ways of relating also include a recognition of the presence of their spouses into the family of origin. This presence brings new challenges and patterns of operating to the young adults' lives. It calls young adults to be connected to their family of origin but also to develop a sense of autonomy, which enables them to establish the uniqueness of their own marital relationship. At this time in their lives, young adults attempt to blend together the traditions and rituals of each of their respective families into a union that captures the riches of both families.

When marriage takes place and a new union begins, each spouse needs to assist the other in integrating the ways of his or her particular family of origin. This is often very difficult because of the family's expectations of the in-law; the family of origin's ability to be open to new members; the placement and role of the young adults in their family of origin; and the in-law's ability to adapt to this new situation. For integration to take place, all these factors need to be recognized.

The young adults also are called to act as mediators between their family of origin and their spouses. Young adults need to be free from being overly identified with their family of origin. This freedom enables them to recognize the fears that may be present because of the changes that have taken place due to the addition of a new member. It will also assist young adults as they assure both their family of origin and their spouses that a new member can be integrated into the family without taking away from the existing relationships. If young adults are able to facilitate successfully this integration, new ways of relating may add richness to all the relationships of this family unit.

New-Parent Stage

As young adults enter into the New-Parent Stage, they take upon a role that is rooted in their own experience of being parented. The major task of this time is to become free to raise their children without trying to show their parents how they "should" have been raised. Until the young adults have come to terms with their own family history, they will constantly engage in activities with their children, not for their children's sake but to prove this unresolved issue. An example of this dynamic would be any obsessive affection or overinvolvement with the children on the part of the parents (e.g., stage father, little-league mother).

The roles and expectations that young adults will have of each other as parents will also be rooted in their positive experiences of being nurtured. Young adults will expect their spouses to play the same roles in parenting their children as their fathers or mothers played in their lives. These expectations may not be realized because of the different characteristics and life experiences of their spouses. Disillusionment and frustration over what is perceived to be lacking in the spouse may cause a strain in the marital relationship. Rather than becoming "stuck" in unrealistic roles and expectations of the spouse, the challenge facing young adults is to identify the values underlying the desired behaviors and to establish new ways of expressing these values.

Patterns of Interaction as Man and Woman

In this section, the young adults' patterns of interaction as man or woman will be explored. These patterns influence how young adults are attracted to others and why this attraction sometimes develops into romantic interest. For the young adults to relate to others as a man or woman, they need to have an understanding of how the images of men and women were projected within their family of origin.

The essence of one's maleness and femaleness is tied to how one experienced the same-sexed parent as man or woman in relationship to the opposite-sexed parent. The identification with the like-sexed parent and the idealization of the opposite-sex parent, in their roles as man and woman, establish how the young adults will develop relationships. As young adults observe their same-sexed parent in relationship with that significant opposite-sexed person, they either identify positively or negatively with that parent.

In a positive identification, young adults like what they see and imitate the behavior of the like-sexed parent. For example, the young man's father was a generous person to his spouse, and the young adult admired that quality. As the young adult develops as a man, the quality of generosity with women becomes an automatic part of his relationship, sometimes to a fault.

In a negative identification, there is a strong dislike for how the same-sexed parent handled the opposite-sexed parent. It is sometimes rooted in an empathetic response to the opposite-sexed parent and an attempt to develop behavior to show the same-sexed parent how one "should" be in relationship. An example of this dynamic would be a young man who observes his father as being unable to stand up and deal creatively with a strong woman, his mother. The young adult, in a negative identification with his father, will invert his father's behavior in order to show him how to handle strong women. In his relationships with women, the young man will then seek to be in control and will be suspicious of being manipulated. He will find it very difficult to be vulnerable or dependent with women for fear that his father's pattern will be repeated in himself.

The behaviors that develop from these unconscious positive or negative identifications are often manifested in affection, nurturance, genital expression, conflict, and anger. Based on their particular identification, it is important for young adults to be aware of the "computer program" that is already in their psyches regarding how they "should" act in their relationships with the opposite sex. In order to take responsibility for how they act and/or respond in relationships, the young adults need to become aware of the compulsive behaviors (e.g., overly generous or independent) that may develop out of the existing "program." They need to see how these behaviors impact on the development of their relationships. Failure to recognize these dynamics will perpetuate patterns of behavior and make it difficult for the young adults to change their behavior, even if this behavior is causing pain in the existing relationships. This inability to take responsibility for their behavior in relationships also causes young adults to blame others and impose unrealistic change on the persons with whom they are involved.

In the idealizing of the opposite-sex parent, young adults will develop certain images and expectations of how the opposite sex "should" be. Young adults will image in an exaggerated form whatever qualities were present in the parent of the opposite sex (e.g., nurturance, abandonment, violence, protection). Therefore, when they encounter someone who possesses these qualities, young adults will react in a driven manner to that experience. Often it is impossible for the opposite sex to live up to these images and expectations because young adults have an exaggerated concept of how these "should" be manifested. For example, if a young man has idealized how his mother nurtured his father, he will look for a woman who possesses that quality. But if this woman exhibits this quality in one hundred different ways, the young adult will want one hundred and ten ways because he has magnified this quality and aggrandized the expectations.

In order to deal with these dynamics, young adults have to realize that their identity as man or woman is rooted in themselves, not in the like-sexed parent. Once this elusive sense of self is realized, young adults can let go of the obsessive need to correct their parent in "how to be" a man or woman in relationship with the opposite sex. Young adults can also be freed from overidentification with the same-sexed parent. This overidentification is rooted in the need of young adults to win acceptance from that like-sexed parent. This approval is based on the fact that by becoming like that parent, one cannot be rejected for who one is (as man or woman). Through this process of overidentification, one knows what it means to be male or female because the parents have accepted themselves in the young adult. This acceptance tells the young adult that how he or she is acting, as man or women, is right.

The following questions may help young adults deal with these dynamics, as well as help them realize to whom they may be attracted:

- What are you trying to show the same-sex parent in his or her relationship with the opposite-sexed person? (Example: how to be independent as a woman.)

- How are you imitating the same-sexed parent in his or her relationship with the opposite-sex person? (Example: to be a woman is to be professional, not a "princess.")

- What qualities of the opposite-sexed parent did you admire that were manifested in relationship with his or her partner? (Example: sensitivity, gentleness, and affection.)

Young adult women with experiences similar to the above examples may be attracted to the following kinds of men. By doing so, they will play out certain internalized programs:

- *Strong Man.* In this choice, she can show her mother how to be independent, even with a strong man. The ironic part about the dynamic is that the woman may inevitably fail and end up creating the same pattern as her mother.

- *Confident Man.* She chooses a man who is not threatened by her as a professional woman and values that quality—but who is also able to help integrate the best parts of being a "princess." A frustration that may take place is that the man may always expect the competent, professional woman and not be able to deal with her vulnerability.

- *Gentle, Affectionate, Sensitive Man.* These qualities may be intensified in the man she chooses and may never be enough because of an aggrandized expectation.

By being aware of the above factors and working through them, mutually, in a self-revelatory fashion, young adults can break the patterns of behavior that have existed from generation to generation in their family of origin. They can now change and choose behaviors that will be life fulfilling and sustaining for their relationships.

Communities of Attraction and Initiation

How the young adults' families dealt with the issues of cohesion and adaptability will determine the kinds of communities to which the young adult will be attracted.

Family Cohesion

"Family cohesion is the emotional bonding that family members have with one another and the relative degree of autonomy a person experiences in a (family) system."[6] A family lives in a dynamic balance between being too connected (*enmeshed*) or too separated (*disengaged*). When a family is enmeshed, the members are not allowed to possess an individual identity other than that of the family's. Members constantly live out the expectations of the family without any appreciation of themselves as unique persons with their own strengths and weaknesses. When a family is disengaged, the individual has little sense of or appreciation for the family as a whole. The person sees no connection between him or herself and other family members. Family members simply coexist in the same space.[7]

If young adults come from families that were primarily enmeshed and did not resist this enmeshment, they will initiate and be attracted to communities in which they can become dependent and subservient. In

[6]Guernsey, p. 101.
[7]P. Carnes, *Family Development I: Understanding Us* (Minneapolis, Minn.: Interpersonal Communications Programs, Inc., 1981), pp. 63-95.

many ways, the community will become a security blanket for the young adults. They will expect all their support from its members and try to do everything in common. Everyone will be expected to reveal who they are, with privacy being considered as a threat to the community. Members will be asked to look, think, and act alike. Decisions will be made by a select few. The young adults will identify with the group to an extreme degree, and anything that threatens the life of the group is likened to a personal attack on each of its members.

If young adults resisted the enmeshment of their families of origin, they will initiate and be attracted to the same kind of group, but will always be considered the outsiders or the "different" ones. They will engage in activities that will show the group how uniquely different they are, but they will still have a strong need to be accepted as a full member of the group. This need will create an inner tension within themselves and place these young adults in a position of always trying to prove to the group that they are worthy of membership.

Disengaged families will produce young adults who have little sense of community. The individual needs of the young adult will always take precedence over the needs of anyone else in the community. They will not seriously consider the sense of responsibility for each other and of making this community happen. There will be hardly any support from each other and self-disclosure among its members will be frowned upon. Very little will be done in common, and identity with the group will be insignificant.

If young adults have resisted the disengagement within their families of origin, they will still be attracted to similar groups, but will have an obsessive need to bring the group together and make it into a community.

They will take over responsibility for the emotional life of the group and manipulate the group to provide support for themselves, as well as engage the group in common activities that, at times, seem artificial.

These examples describe the extreme polarities that exist within the issue of family cohesion. Young adults will fall somewhere on the continuum, with a tendency toward one of the extremes.

Family Adaptability

Adaptability is the ability of a system to change its structure, including its power of affiliations, its role definitions, and its relationship rules in order to be responsive to situational and cultural stresses. Families live in a dynamic balance between being too structured (*rigid*) or too flexible (*chaotic*).[8]

When a family is too structured, individual members are not open to change or input. The emphasis is on maintaining the status quo of relating and operating as family. Change is difficult and is faced with much resistance. When a family is too flexible, individual members are constantly exposed to unmitigated change. The structure is fluid and unstable.[9]

If young adults come from homes that are primarily rigid, they will initiate or be attracted to groups that are dictatorial in nature. The agenda of the group will be cast in stone and will be fiercely defended. They will be overly organized and problems will be addressed simplistically. Their values or code of behavior will be adhered to religiously. Persons who express a different value or behavior will be ostracized.

[8]K. M. Galvin and B. J. Brommel, *Family Communication: Cohesion and Change,* second ed. (Glenview, Ill.: Scott, Foresman & Co., 1986), p. 14.
[9]Guernsey, p. 101.

If the young adults resisted the rigidity of their households, they will still initiate or be attracted to a similar group but will become "Peck's Bad Boy." They will challenge the group's limits in a way that doesn't destroy themselves or the group. They will be accepted by the group, but will always be regarded with a certain amount of suspicion and/or lack of trust.

A family that is chaotic will produce young adults who have a difficult time in dealing with any kind of structure. The structure will be free-wheeling with very little restraints; problems will never be resolved and things will "just happen." Their values will be so free-flowing that the group will be unable to focus on anything specific in which to believe or engage.

If the young adults have resisted the chaotic experience of their families of origin, they will still initiate or be attracted to similar groups, but will seek to put limits on the group. The young adults will take over responsibility for solving the problems of individual members or of the group as a whole. They will attempt to persuade each member to believe in some specific goal and accomplish some kind of task. They will have an intense need to make this group work.

Young adults will need to have an appreciation of how their families of origin dealt with the issues of cohesion and adaptability. It will also be important for the young adults to have an understanding of the roles that they played within their families in dealing with these issues. The key question for young adults is whether they went along with or resisted the family's expression of cohesion and adaptability. An understanding of how they responded will begin to help young adults see how they operate in a group. This knowledge will begin to free them so that they can decide how they wish to interact with a particular group versus playing their indigenous roles. This understanding will also help young adults initiate or be engaged with other groups that operate differently from that to which they have been accustomed.

This knowledge is also of great value for leaders who work with young adults. By becoming aware of the dynamics of their own families of origin, the leaders will have an understanding of why they are setting up the group in a certain fashion and why they are attracting certain kinds of young adults to their ministry.

Young Adults as Change Agents

Young adults play a unique role in helping their family of origin break patterns of relationship that have existed for generations. "Change by one member challenges the roles and rules by which one's family operates and causes stress that requires one's family either to maintain its status quo or to adjust to the change."[10] The task of the young adults in this process will be a difficult one depending upon how open or closed to change their families of origin are. Young adults cannot undertake this task alone. They need the help of a supportive community in which they can reflect on how their family of origin relates. This community can help young adults deal with the natural judgmental stance that arises when one begins to look at one's family of origin.

There is the tendency among individuals to begin to think in terms of good or bad regarding the experience of one's family of origin. This supportive community can facilitate the art of looking at one's family of origin so that young adults can see and appreciate what *was*.

---

[10]*A Family Perspective*, p. 26.

This contemplation can initiate young adults into a healing and reconciliation process that will free them to understand and accept profoundly the story of their family of origin and its individual members. It will break through the unrealistic as well as unmet expectations that young adults have in their hearts regarding how their family "should" have been for them.

This freedom will also help young adults to have the ability to decide how they wish to enter relationship versus being in relationships based on the old "computer" program. Young adults will begin to see anew the unique mystery of every person who now enters their lives. Out of this vision, young adults will be able to enter in and touch the very depth of another. This touch alone will open others to new ways of relating.

In order to facilitate this healing and reconciling process in ministry to and with young adults, leaders in the Church need to engage in the following recommendations.

"[I]t is important that leaders, together with the individual (young adults) in the program, determine the following:

- How the individual's family is currently operating.
- How the individual's family addresses the issues of cohesion and adaptability.
- What roles the individual plays within his or her family, as well as the patterns of interaction.
- How open his or her family is to change.
- How the individual's change will affect his or her family and its members.
- What other family members would support the individual's change and help the family change its ways of relating and of assigning roles.

- What skills and knowledge may be needed by the family in order to change in response to the individual's change."[11]

As church ministers engage with young adults in viewing and changing their responses to their family of origin, and other significant relationships, the young adults' families themselves may have courage to embark on a journey that will open for them new ways of living.

---

[11]Ibid., p. 27.

Hispanic Young Adult Ministry

Ms. Armantina R. Pelaez

The ministry to Hispanic young adults gives us an opportunity to be participants in building bridges from the past to the present. This ministerial call requires a commitment to justice and love. It is rooted in the ancestral traditions of women and men struggling to preserve their value and dignity as people of God. This human drama never really ends, but the plot remains essentially the same struggle as that of their ancestors. What has changed are the numerous reasons for immigration and the process of adapting to being a Hispanic American, a New York Puerto Rican, a Chicano, or a Latin American in the United States.

In this chapter, we are focusing on only one segment of the Hispanic ministry mosaic—Hispanic young adults. Hispanic youth and young adults make up 54 percent of the total Hispanic population. Hispanics are a growing population in the United States, with a median age in 1980 of twenty-three, compared to thirty-one for the non-Hispanic population.[1] Therefore, the Hispanic young adult population is not one to be ignored. They are a people rich with gifts, culture, heritage, and traditions. But they are a people in need of

---

[1] U.S. Department of Commerce Bureau of the Census, 1985. *Persons of Spanish-Speaking Origin in the U.S.: March 1985.* Current Population Reports Series, p. 20, no. 403.

guidance, ministry, and healing. As ministers to and with Hispanic young adults it is important to keep all these factors in mind as this ministry is developed.

Who Are the Hispanic Young Adults?

Just as the dominant culture is vague in defining young adults, we as Hispanics also have great difficulty in defining who we are. The National Committee of Hispanic Youth and Young Adult Ministry, which originated from the *II Encuentro Nacional Hispano de Pastoral* in 1977, does not have a defined age group for this ministry. They speak of the relationship between youth and young adults as an integrated component of the ministry. So their ages range from preadolescence through mid-thirties, but no clear definition is given to the relationships among the particular age groups. There is a recognition of the developmental differences between the age groups, but there is no time to philosophize on the theory. The ministry needs are urgent, and reality forces ministry to take place without a focus on the spiritual and psychological differences.

The Hispanic young adults are immigrants from Latin America, Central America, the Caribbean, and South America; they are refugees, illegal aliens, and migrant workers. Many of them are first, second, and third generations of Hispanic ancestors. Some are bilingual or multilingual, while others are only monolingual in English or Spanish.

Hispanic young adults have as much difficulty reflecting on their life crises and situations as on the integrating aspect of developmental stages addressed by psychology. An everyday crisis is view by them as an integrated aspect of life rather than as a transitional stage from one particular age to another. Many parish, diocesan, and regional personnel treat the Hispanic young adult as just another "adult," primarily because so many of them have established families and have children of their own. A large number of the Hispanic "early" young adults are in the work force on a full-time basis. Many of them hold a part-time job on the side to make ends meet and to support their immediate and extended families. Others struggle to attend college at night or on weekends. Hispanic young adults are impoverished by the realities of both urban and rural life. Among young migrant farm workers, basic education is a luxury beyond their reach.

In 1984, the population of Hispanic families falling below the poverty line was more than twice that of non-Hispanic families—25 percent versus 11 percent—according to figures released by the U.S. Department of Commerce in 1985. Hispanic young adults' gender, education, and age have an impact on the labor force. The social expectations regarding gender roles in marriage and family formation, especially in the early teenage years (early young adult period) hinder many women from obtaining work experience during those years.

Hispanic Young Adults and Family Ministry

The Hispanic young adults face realities similar to many young adults in our society. Most Hispanic young adults marry at a very early age. Early marriage among Hispanic youth needs to be understood within the cultural context. Many get married so early in life because of a false concept that in the late-twenties, he or she has a slim chance of finding a spouse. Moreover, a Hispanic woman has less chance than a man because at that age she is considered old; this is a fact of the culture. A large number of these young people enter into marriage without adequate preparation for this life commitment. Many of these young adult couples are supported emotionally, spiritually, and, at times, economically by parents and extended families. It is the woman who is considered to be responsible for the maintenance of the relationship and for carrying on their family goals.

As a minister, I was challenged by a Peruvian young adult, whom I will call José. José, like many other Hispanic males, was pushed into a "Latin lover" image at a very early age, principally through sexual talk and adventuring. Throughout his life, his success has been measured in terms of sexual potential. He came to the United States at the age of fourteen and became acculturated by the dominant culture of New York regionalism. José completed college and found himself an excellent job in the banking industry. He met a woman—a Peruvian illegal alien—and married her, despite his family's opposition to the marriage. His wife was without any significant exposure to the dominant culture. She found José's view of Catholic norms in opposition to her own upbringing as a Catholic in Peru. Their sexual relationship become an issue of control in light of their understanding of female virginity and masculine virility. After seeking professional assistance, their marriage was consummated.

They are now expecting a child after only a brief period of married life. Problems began with the extended family right after her pregnancy was announced. José's in-laws were expected to share the burden and assist Maria in her later months of pregnancy. José's resentments toward his in-laws were aggravated by prior tensions in the marriage. The child was to be named after José's parents. Naming the baby became a point of contention between the spouses since José's parents were against the marriage from the very beginning. He was challenged by her on his physical strength and courage and by her expectations of his career. Success has been measured as an aspect of his virility.

With many in the Hispanic culture, family formation, boundary problems, and loyalty conflicts within the families are common. The relationship between daughter-in-law and mother-in-law is crucial for the success of the marriage. The daughter-in-law is expected to have the same obligations as a daughter and to perform many household chores under the supervision of her mother-in-law. Most young women, particularly those raised in the United States, no longer tolerate this role. Consequently, marital and family conflict arise in light of cultural values. Motherly love is held at a much higher regard than wifely love, creating resentment between spouses. The role of mother is idealized and equated with self-denial.

José's stress has been inflicted by his wife's uncles; they encourage him to think about the possibility of having extramarital affairs. His moral norms do not agree that marital problems can be resolved by engaging in extramarital affairs. Her uncles talk freely about their affairs; it is considered quite proper. It is common for a Hispanic male to have a mistress and to have children by her. José knows that the culture's values are in conflict with his moral norms of being Catholic and a

Hispanic male who grew up in the United States. The more the marriage has difficulties, the more he has attempted to fall into the cultural value of extramarital affairs.

José's conflicts represent just some of the issues that ministers need to address in Hispanic young adult ministry. One important element in ministering to Hispanic young adults is to integrate that ministry with family life ministries and family catechesis. The understanding of the family's norms, traditions, and values offers us an opportunity to minister to Hispanic young adults in the building of a meaningful parish community.

Religion and Culture

The research of Gonzalez and La Velle (1985) looked at Hispanic youth's Mass attendance.[2] The respondents, eighteen to twenty-nine years old, indicated that they attended Mass regularly. Those under eighteen attended Mass regularly either with family or friends, or even alone. Youth from the Dominican Republic, Ecuador, Honduras, Mexico, Puerto Rico, and Salvador attended on a more regular basis than those from Colombia, Cuba, Guatemala, Nicaragua, Peru, and Spain. Also American-born youth from Catholic Hispanic descendants were slightly more likely to attend Mass regularly than foreign-born Catholic Hispanic youth. These slight differences need to be researched further in light of the popular practices of the adult Hispanic spirituality. In addition, the research revealed that the higher the in-

[2]Roberto O. Gonzalez and Michael La Velle, *The Hispanic Catholic in the United States: A Socio, Cultural and Religious Profile* (New York: Northeast Catholic Pastoral Center for Hispanics, 1985), p. 90.

come in the family, the higher the percentage of regular Mass attendance by the Hispanic youth. What impact does this study have on Hispanic young adult ministry? The impact of affluence versus poverty within the Hispanic communities needs to be addressed in parish programs.

Many Hispanic ministers, religious educators, and catechists give considerable attention to the issue of culture, but very often they focus on the positive and enrichment aspects of culture within Hispanic ministry. An element that needs to be fostered among ministers and religious educators, however, is the cultivation of Hispanic piety among families. Acculturation and the importance of religion and its relationship to culture need to be articulated further in the ministry.

Pelaez (1987) explored the six stages in crosscultural young adult ministry: (1) dissonance, tolerance, and self-consciousness; (2) militancy and pride; (3) acceptance; (4) a bicultural identity; (5) a multicultural identity process; and (6) promotion of openness and communication needed in a ministry to young adults.[3] The relationship of these stages to Hispanic young adults needs to be integrated into parish youth and young adult ministry programs. The tension among second-generation Hispanic young adults relates to educational, geographical, and economical factors.

The length of the experience in the dominant culture is an important variable in determining the degree of assimilation to the dominant culture. How does this degree of assimilation versus an acculturation process

---

[3]Armantina Pelaez, "Multicultural Dimensions of Young Adult Ministry," *Young Adult Ministry: A Book of Readings,* edited by Ron Bagley, CJM (Naugatuck, Conn.: Center for Youth Ministry Development, 1987), pp. 51-58.

determine the religious expressions among Hispanic young adults?

Hispanic Cultural Values

In order to assist in ministering to Hispanic young adults, the following are some common Hispanic cultural values. It is important to be aware of these values in order to respond effectively in this ministerial call. However, *objectivity* needs to be incorporated as the main principle in ministry. These cultural trends might vary from young adult to young adult; from one Hispanic ethnic group to another Hispanic ethnic group. Consequently, background information needs to be taken into account, not generalizations or stereotypes:

- In the Hispanic culture, the nuclear family is embedded in an extended family. Children who are orphaned or whose parents are divorced are included in the household of relatives, along with adults who have remained single, widowed, or divorced. The children's grandparents or *compadres* are often considered to be part of the extended family. Close friends are called "uncle" or "aunt" by the children.[4]

- Dependence is encouraged. Affiliation and cooperation are stressed, while confrontation and competition are discouraged.

- Personalism is the focus on relationships rather than tasks.

- Loyalty to the family of origin is expected. Honesty and the preservation of one's dignity is a funda-

---

[4]O. Paz, *The Labyrinth of Solitude: Life and Thought in Mexico* (New York: Evergreen Books, 1961).

mental value. *Pobre pero honesto*—poor but honest—is a value of the highest order.

- Maldonado Sierra and Trent (1960) observed that Hispanic women may rebel against the role of submission to men by expressing passive aggression and manipulation of the males in their families.[5] For example, a woman who discovers that her husband is having an extramarital affair may refuse to have sexual intercourse with him, complaining of body aches and nervousness.

- The ideal of manliness or virility dictates that men be aggressive, sexually experienced, courageous, and protective of their women (including mother, sisters, and wives) and their children. The female ideal is to be humble, submissive, virtuous, and devoted to home and children. Stevens (1973) uncovers the female power in the centrality of the self-sacrificing mother.[6]

- Respect for authority is learned at home. For instance, Puerto Ricans think that a child who calls an adult by his or her first name without using *"Dona," "Señor,"* or *"Señora"* is disrespectful. To make direct eye contact with strangers, especially women and children, is also unacceptable.

- Women, are encouraged to emulate the Virgin Mary. Pressure for female purity is reinforced by religious ideology. Women are taught to repress or sublimate their sexual drives and usually regard sex as an obligation. They are trained to be ex-

---

[5]E. Maldonado Sierra and R. D. Trent, "Neuroses and Traditional Beliefs in Puerto Rico," *International Journal of Social Psychiatry* 6 (1960): 237.

[6]E. Stevens, "Marianismo: The Other Face of Machismo" in A. Pescatello (ed.), *Female and Male in Latin American* (Pittsburgh: University of Pittsburgh Press, 1973).

tremely modest, which often leads to shame about their bodies. Intimate relations are not discussed openly, even with priests or therapists. As a result, childrearing patterns emphasize protecting girls to ensure their innocence until marriage. The traditional practice of *chaperonas* during courtship is maintained by some Hispanic families. A young woman's rebellion against the traditions of *chaperonas* may be viewed as a signal of conflicts between the mother and daughter. Virginity is a difficult issue that needs to be addressed in young adult ministry in light of the acculturation process.

- The acculturation process of Hispanic women in the work force has created a great deal of conflict among spouses. How have men adapted to women working, rather than fulfilling their traditional role of being home? How are the children affected by the changes of family traditions? These are complex questions that need to be addressed by family ministers, marriage encounters, engagement encounters, and family catechesis.

Pastoral Recommendations

Ministry to Hispanic young adults needs to take into consideration their own Hispanic ethnic backgrounds: the exposure to the dominant culture; the acculturation process of the individual within the cultural transitions; the second-generation tensions of being a Hispanic American; the creations and patterns arising from exposure to the dominant culture and life cycle.

Ministry to Hispanic young adults needs to focus on issues that can cause entanglements within families.

One of these issues, which can be critical, is when the relationship of family members is threatened by the fear that young adults will be lost to a new set of values and norms. In another example, the conflict between younger and older generations may precipitate severe problems within the family. The key to ministering to Hispanic young adults is learning, understanding, and accepting the cultural transitions as a process of acculturation.

And finally, perhaps one of the most important aspects of ministry to Hispanic young adults can be found in the *National Catechetical Directory* (n. 194): "At all times, catechesis must respect the personal dignity of minority group members, avoiding condescension and patronizing attitudes."

What Young Adults May Expect of Their Church

Human life is subject to constant change, from birth through maturity and old age. Therefore, we must be able to provide a ministry for all of life, not just particular segments. It must have something to support the child, to excite the youth, to challenge the young adult, to fortify the middle adult, and to enrich and sustain the life of old age.

To be more specific, young adults have a right to expect—as do those persons in any age group—that their Church will support and sustain them in their human and spiritual needs. This right grows out of the needs and nature of every young adult. Certain basic elements are required in providing the life, growth, and maturing into full personhood. If fulfillment of these basic needs can be achieved, then the Church will be well on the way to providing a truly adequate ministry to young adults.

It is all well and good to speak in terms of general needs, but only by pinpointing certain real, identifiable objectives can we really begin ministry with these young persons. Following is a list of elements that time and experience have proven most essential to this ministry. The local ministry must strive to create a relaxed setting in which young adults can:

- learn and live out a Christian life;
- share and test images and ideas;

- learn how to cope with futility and how to change despair into hope;
- know how new spiritual life begins and how it is regenerated;
- learn how to develop an adequate self-image;
- learn to deal with questions concerning sexuality and sex;
- make use of opportunities for leadership training and development and assume leadership responsibilities;
- know themselves in relationship to God, other persons, and society;
- learn to make decisions in light of their Christian faith;
- learn to cope with acceptance and rejection;
- further their own growth before God; and
- identify what it means to be a man, a woman, a child of God.

Areas of Religious Need

Young adults identify the following as important religious needs:

Liturgy

They want Sunday Mass to make a difference in their lives, and it is on this basis that they will continue to go. There is an apparent need for more young adult liturgies in some parishes. There is a need for young adults to be lectors and participate in planning liturgies. Many feel that they are left out of things in the parish or community. They complain about the quality of the homilies. They feel that they are boring, irrelevant, and sometimes nothing but a long commercial for money. There is need for liturgical leadership and homilistic skills in parishes.

Pre-Cana

While they state that the Pre-Cana program is answering some needs, there are those who want a more extensive program. We need to prepare people for relationships in significant ways.

Moral Decision Making

There are moral, social, and ethical issues where some look to the Church to assist in decision making. What they want more than answers is the opportunity to air openly and thoroughly their views and questions. Hence, the great need for discussion groups for young adults at the parish level.

Communal Prayer

A small number in this age group are looking for communal prayer life, a more personal kind of prayer than Sunday Eucharist. Some are finding the charismatic movement rather appealing. Establishing communal prayer programs in some areas may fulfill that need.

Bible Study

An increasing number of young adults want to know about Jesus and his times and feel that parishes should provide discussion groups or classes in Scripture. Some pastors maintain that there are parishes with these programs, but that young adults do not attend.

Social Action

For many young adults, religion is largely a matter of helping one's neighbor. Most people do this independently of any relationship with the Church, and in fact, some state that they find no leadership in the Church in this area. Some young adults are willing to respond to appeals for active involvement in social issues made by the Church.

Coffee Shops or Centers

Many young adults feel that parishes should provide local or regional coffee shops or centers where they could drop in and meet with their peers, elders, and religious leaders or participate in discussion groups, counseling, and social activities. Young adults believe that there should be someone who is always available—someone who would take an interest in them—when they are seeking help or simply need to talk.

Counseling

There is a great need for priests, sisters, and lay people who are professionally trained in counseling. The history of the Church in the United States shows that priests and religious have not been prepared for counseling and that most of the counseling in parishes has been nothing but authoritarian directives. There is a need for professionals who can listen patiently and then use the right counseling techniques; this is especially true in the area of drug and alcoholic abuse counseling.

Religious Education

Evangelization is lifting up and expanding the faith; it is all of life. Some form of religious education that is appealing and suited to young adult needs should be offered.

Participation

Many young adults feel that they are left out of parish/church planning and activities. They want to be invited to serve as lectors, as members of the parish council or parish planning committee, and so forth. Unless more direct and personal invitations are made to young adults, it is doubtful if they will come forth on their own.

Retreats

Young adults claim that more effort should be made to provide retreats for them. For those who cannot go away for two days, perhaps a day of recollection can be offered. They state that too many retreats are either institutionally related (e.g., high schools, colleges, etc.) or that the retreats are not geared to them and are, consequently, irrelevant.

Conclusion

Although the task may seem overwhelming at times, we encourage all church leaders to continue to develop ministry "for and with" young adults. We applaud the efforts of those who have advocated for young adults. We hope that these forgotten people—young adults— will come to be recognized for their gifts, talents, and needs.